# The Joke

by **Sam Marks**

FOUNDED 1830

NEW YORK HOLLYWOOD LONDON TORONTO

SAMUELFRENCH.COM

Copyright © 2009 by Sam Marks

ALL RIGHTS RESERVED

CAUTION: Professionals and amateurs are hereby warned that *THE JOKE* is subject to a royalty. It is fully protected under the copyright laws of the United States of America, the British Commonwealth, including Canada, and all other countries of the Copyright Union. All rights, including professional, amateur, motion picture, recitation, lecturing, public reading, radio broadcasting, television and the rights of translation into foreign languages are strictly reserved. In its present form the play is dedicated to the reading public only.

The amateur live stage performance rights to *THE JOKE* are controlled exclusively by Samuel French, Inc., and royalty arrangements and licenses must be secured well in advance of presentation. PLEASE NOTE that amateur royalty fees are set upon application in accordance with your producing circumstances. When applying for a royalty quotation and license please give us the number of performances intended, dates of production, your seating capacity and admission fee. Royalties are payable one week before the opening performance of the play to Samuel French, Inc., at 45 W. 25th Street, New York, NY 10010.

Royalty of the required amount must be paid whether the play is presented for charity or gain and whether or not admission is charged.

Stock royalty quoted upon application to Samuel French, Inc.

For all other rights than those stipulated above, apply to: SUBIAS, One Union Square West, #913, New York, NY 10003, Attn: Mark Subias.

Particular emphasis is laid on the question of amateur or professional readings, permission and terms for which must be secured in writing from Samuel French, Inc.

Copying from this book in whole or in part is strictly forbidden by law, and the right of performance is not transferable.

Whenever the play is produced the following notice must appear on all programs, printing and advertising for the play: "Produced by special arrangement with Samuel French, Inc."

Due authorship credit must be given on all programs, printing and advertising for the play.

ISBN 978-0-573-66333-8    Printed in U.S.A.    #12664

No one shall commit or authorize any act or omission by which the copyright of, or the right to copyright, this play may be impaired.

No one shall make any changes in this play for the purpose of production.

Publication of this play does not imply availability for performance. Both amateurs and professionals considering a production are strongly advised in their own interests to apply to Samuel French, Inc., for written permission before starting rehearsals, advertising, or booking a theatre.

No part of this book may be reproduced, stored in a retrieval system, or transmitted in any form, by any means, now known or yet to be invented, including mechanical, electronic, photocopying, recording, videotaping, or otherwise, without the prior written permission of the publisher.

### IMPORTANT BILLING AND CREDIT REQUIREMENTS

All producers of *THE JOKE must* give credit to the Author of the Play in all programs distributed in connection with performances of the Play, and in all instances in which the title of the Play appears for the purposes of advertising, publicizing or otherwise exploiting the Play and/or a production. The name of the Author *must* appear on a separate line on which no other name appears, immediately following the title and *must* appear in size of type not less than fifty percent of the size of the title type.

World Premiere Studio Dante (NYC) October 17th – November 2007
Directed by Sam Gold

***THE JOKE*** premiered at Studio Dante on October 20, 2007 in New York City. The production was directed by Sam Gold, the assistant director was Noel Allain, and was produced by Michael & Victoria Imperioli, Tina Thor, and Howard Axel with the following cast:

DOUG . . . . . . . . . . . . . . . . . . . . . . . . . . . . . . . . . . . . . Jordan Gelber
ED . . . . . . . . . . . . . . . . . . . . . . . . . . . . . . . . . . . . . Thomas Sadoski

Scenic & Costume Design - Victoria Imperioli
Lighting Design - Tony Giovannetti
Sound Design - David Margolin Lawson
Consultant - Jerry Grayson
Master Carpenter - Ryczard Chlebowski
Stage Manager - Darren Rosen
Assistant Stage Manager - Devon Butler
Dramaturg - Francine Volpe
Artwork Design - Nathanial Kilcer
Photography - George Mclaughlin
Casting by - Jack Doulin
Casting Assistant - Jenn Haltman
Press Representative - The KarpEl Group

## AUTHOR'S NOTE

The action of this play occurs in the Catskills from 1965 to 1973. One can track the progression of time by the mention of certain political events (Watts, Nixon) as well as the evolution of Doug's marriage (date, marry, child). Scene to scene, year to year, backstage to on-stage all should bleed into each other. No blackouts, please.

To the actors:

–Play this for the speed of a joke. Always moving forward.

–Know when you're being funny and know when you're not being funny.

–Listen to your father (or grandfather) tell jokes; sometimes they are all that he can say.

–Listen to your little brother tell jokes; that mean and that gross.

–There are many comedians from the era to admire but for specific influences you might want to watch Dean Martin, Jerry Lewis, Lenny Bruce, and Bob Newhart.

*(Here's what was left behind:*

*The Beach. The boardwalk. Showing off a picture from the newspaper to Mom. Showing it off to friends. The roar of their laughter. Imitating the TV. Practicing in the living room.*

*Here's where we are now:*

*The Catskills. Summer 1965.*

*Lakes not beaches.*

*A very different kind of laughter.*

*Rum and coke, whiskey highball, gin martini, and headache in the morning.*

*Eat, talk, plan, practice, and then backstage smoking and waiting to go on.*

*On stage now:*

*The face makeup.*

*The pomade.*

*A newspaper.*

*A hat and a drum.*

*A Velvet Curtain.*

*We are in the dressing room.*

*Warm Yellow Light.*

*A mirror.*

**DOUG** *and* **ED** *are warming up, getting ready to go on.)*

**DOUG.** (*setting up a joke*) Was it *Big*? Was it *Big*?

**ED.** Here we go.

(**ED** *fixes his hair,* **DOUG** *pulls up his pants.*)

**DOUG.** (*Ramping up again*) You know, the drinks here are really big.

I had a drink last night and the glass was *so big*.
This glass was *so big*.

I can't – I can't do it.

**ED.** You gotta.

**DOUG.** I can't.

**ED.** (*big warm smile*) Hey, you're golden!
Cunt.

**DOUG.** (*setting it up again*) Okay, okay. Here I go.
Wheeeeeew.
The glass was *So Big*
It was *So Big*
I gave Lola a sip and she fell in.
She hasn't been seen since.

I got worried about her so I called the Coast Guard.

Where's Lola? *She's in the glass!*

(*explaining the joke*)

Short girl – big glass.

**ED.** (*total deadpan*) That's really Wonderful.

**DOUG.** Okay okay:
This glass was *so big* the bartender didn't stir the drink he *drained it.*

**ED.** Good…

**DOUG.** I don't wanna say the glass was big but thank God I'm a strong swimmer.
C'mon Eddie – *that's* good stuff.

**ED.** Certainly is Doug it most certainly is

**DOUG.** Awwww Shucksey Wuksey Eddie – ya just saying that!

**ED.** I haven't laughed that hard since you told me about those German camps with the funny names.

(*a beat*)

**DOUG.** Well we can't all be the Cowboy of Comedy you are.
Walking off stage, riding into the sunset. Yah yah yah ye-haa!

Your pockets *stuffed* with 10 dollars, a used condom, some brisket and a menorah ya lifted off some Jewish broad named Arlene.

**ED.** It's true, I can't get enough of the Jews:

Their women, their brisket, and their gold – especially from the teeth.

**DOUG.** (*mock upset*) Hey those are my people Eddie. My people!

And if ya gonna come up here to the woods and scam them like this

Sleep with the women and eat their food

I think ya owe it to us to tell us how you actually feel about us Christ Killers.

You know     Tell us.

Out of the goodness of your stone cold Irish-Dego heart.

**ED.** You're right about that Dougie, you are.

**DOUG.** You're gonna break some hearts when they find out you actually hate us.

**ED.** Course you won't mind when I ride off.

**DOUG.** (*mock surprise*) Me? No. Me?

I got a little celebration planned for your departure.

Little violins, little tubas, little little little.

**ED.** Judas.

**DOUG.** (*like he's grabbing some breasts*) More girls for the Fatman!

**ED.** What about Lola?

**DOUG.** (*like he doesn't know*) Who's Lola?

Oooohhhhhhhhhh Lola! Right Lola.

She drowned.

**ED.** In the drink. That's good.

**DOUG.** (*enthused*) I'm heartbroken: My girlfriend killed by a rum and coke or as you like to say a Cuba Libre!

**ED.** You're devastated you are.

**DOUG.** (*trying to start a routine*) You'll miss her too, won't you Ed?

**ED.** I got other things going on.

**DOUG.** Oh I know why you won't miss her

**ED.** (*setting up*) And why's that Doug?

**DOUG.** Cause of that thing you got with Maurice, the dishwasher.

**ED.** (*Picking up on the bit*) Maurice is a really good kisser.

**DOUG.** He's got that long tongue.

**ED.** Good for the balls

**DOUG.** (*proud*) I taught him that trick

**ED.** Family tradition?

*(They are amused with themselves.*

**DOUG** *puts on his make-up.)*

**DOUG.** (*dropping the jokes*) Where were you last night?

**ED.** You know me Doug. In early.

**DOUG.** What's her name?

*(**ED** makes the 'jerking off' gesture)*

**DOUG.** I waited for you. All alone, Like one of these sad guys
Drink in my hand, Looking over my shoulder, trying not to cry…

**ED.** You had your Lola.

**DOUG.** I couldn't find her Ed – she drown.

**ED.** Right, right. Big drink.

**DOUG.** (*serious again*) I started writing some new stuff.
On bar napkins.

**ED.** Any good?

**DOUG.** It was so good I threw up on it. The best stuff right next to some old piece of spaghetti.

**ED.** Yeah you're the best man.

**DOUG.** You're not so bad yourself. Although, we forget sometimes cause you do the Alcatraz routine:
Sitting there with a cigarette, waiting for the word from the warden.

**ED.** Yeah. Well. You know. Storing up.

(**DOUG** *sits down and looks at* **ED.**)

**DOUG.** (*as if concerned*) I don't know Ed, *these days…*

**ED.** What?

**DOUG.** You're a little…

(*Doug does the 'Retard' face: eyes crossed, teeth out, lips distorted.*)

**ED.** You serious?

(*Doug still has retard face on.*)

**DOUG.** I do a crossword faster than you can come up with a joke.
And I can't read.

**ED.** (*very direct*) Doug no-one thinks you're funny. No-one.

**DOUG.** It's not that you're slow, you just have really pretty toys.

**ED.** Doug when I told the manager I wanted to bring my partner up here for the summer he said fine but it better not be that fat guy who makes my kids cry.

**DOUG.** (*picks up on the bit*) I tried not rattle the child's crib.

**ED.** But your flask – it bangs against the bars.

**DOUG.** (*an honest defense*) I thought a drink would help calm the kid down, you know, make everything a little easier.

**ED.** Like your Mom used to do for you. Before a bath and a nap.

**DOUG.** (*a little uncomfortable*) Hey, hey, hey.

**ED.** Give and take give and take.

**DOUG.** (*a joke*) Hold on
Are we still talking about Lola        BING!

**ED.** Classic material.

(*Doug pacing.*)

**DOUG.** (*serious again*) Lola's allright, yeah?

**ED.** Whatta mean.

**DOUG.** You don't think she's I don't know.
Like crazy or ugly or dumb or –

**ED.** She's a Beautiful girl. Beautiful girl. You gonna do the right thing by her?

**DOUG.** Next week, I'm takin her to the movies.

**ED.** Wish I could say I had someone.
Bears are looking good to me.

**DOUG.** Well if you want me to put on the skirt just say so.

**ED.** Don't joke around about that.

**DOUG.** Me? Joke? What?

*(They're ready.*

*Drum roll.*

*Lights.*

*Music.)*

**ED.** Here we go.

*(Doug goes onto The Stage.*

*He is now performing before an audience.)*

**DOUG.** Ladies and gentlemen, ladies and gentlemen!
Welcome welcome welcome to the Catskills and welcome to our show!

*(to an audience member)*

No no wait don't leave – we've got prizes, big prizes.
A night with me.
Get it? Big Prizes *(referring to his fatness)*

*(He 'waits for laughter')*

Okay okay now we've got a great comedian for you to see tonight, a good friend of mine, allow me to introduce to Steady Eddie from Bayridge!

*(Ed on stage now.*

*Doug walks to his Drum.*

*Ed speaks to the audience.)*

**ED.** *(referring to Doug)* Hey Dougie stay away from the

microphone please, I know it looks tasty but we only have one.

**DOUG.** Ed, I wasn't gonna eat the mike.

**ED.** *(a joke)* So you're dieting now?

*(Doug gets on his drum.*

*Ed gets in another one.)*

**ED.** I'm not saying Doug eats a lot there there's a buffet back there that's in trauma

**DOUG.** *(setting Ed up)* Ed, you callin me fat?

**ED.** *(innocent)* You? Fat? Of course not!

*(Ed smirks to the audience)*

**ED.** I'm not saying Doug's fat but he sure gets along well with popcorn.

**DOUG.** Oh!

**ED.** I'm not saying he's fat but when he makes love to his girlfriend she needs to take out insurance.

**DOUG.** HEY!

**ED.** I'm just kidding about Doug
He's not fat at all.
Not at All

*(Looks at Doug. Holds.)*

You know you can't eat those drumsticks right?

*(Doug hits a rim shot.)*

*Doug and Ed are on their game.)*

**ED.** Hello there ladies and gentlemen hello.
I love performing here, I hate crowds.

*(Rim shot)*

I've missed you folks I have.

*(Ed looks to a woman in the audience, flirty.)*

Ms. Katz, your husband back? We'll talk later.

*(Rim Shot)*

I don't know what to say. It's wonderful here.

It's summer and Romance is in the air.
These love struck kids come up here.
I hope they have a hose to clean it up.

*(Rim shot.)*

It's crazy all the love up here. Just crazy.
Last night there was a girl knocking on my door all night. About 4'o clock I finally got disgusted. I let her out.

*(Rim shot.)*

There are lots of beautiful Jewish Girls.
Beautiful Jewish Girls.
I can't wait to see some of em.

*(Rim shot.)*

**ED.** I had a Jewish Girlfriend once, I did.
She was a sweet Jewish girl.
And this girl, you know I thought she liked me but really
she broke my heart.
She said
"Come on over     there's no-body home"
I went on over     there was no-body home.

*(Rim shot.)*

This girl, the thing is she liked to entertain.
She had this very good friend.
A very nice guy.
He took the door not the window.

*(Rim shot.)*

Actually if you must know he was a Chinese guy and I walk in on them and he's looking for something.

(**ED** *does the Chinese guy 'looking for his penis' bit.*

*Heavy accent, ugly, racist.*)

"Whera is it?
Wher it go?

Ohhhh.
Dere it is."

*(Back to his voice.)*

Course I looking for my chop suey!

*(Rim shot.)*

**ED.** I cut the girl lose.
Couldn't take it anymore.
I do feel sorry for the next guy she's with.
Hey wait a second!

*(Ed makes a face.)*

Doug, how is your girlfriend?

**DOUG.** Wait?
Are you saying that my girlfriend isn't faithful?

**ED.** I'm saying don't order any Chinese Food.
That guy really delivers.

*(Rim shot.)*

**ED.** Thanks so much ladies and gentleman.
It's been great.
Tomorrow night is young mother's night.
So if any of you ladies are interested in becoming young mothers check with us after the show.

*(Music.*

**DOUG** *and* **ED** *are back in the dressing room.*

**ED** *fixes his hair,* **DOUG** *pulls up his pants.*

**DOUG** *turns to* **ED.***)*

**DOUG.** We gotta talk. It's very important. About the routine. Okay?
First of all: I gotta get more to do.
Second of all and *most importantly,*
You know that th –

*(***DOUG** *mouths something silently while* **ED** *tries to 'listen.')*

**ED.** What?

*(**DOUG** makes gestures while moving his mouth.*

*It's a sight gag.*

*This goes on for a while.)*

**ED.** *(a little annoyed)* Good stuff Doug.

**DOUG.** How do you do that to your face?

**ED.** What's that?

**DOUG.** How do you do what you do to your face?

**ED.** You reek, Doug. They got rules here you know. About that. Sign says. None of that. Back here.

**DOUG.** "Sign says"

**ED.** It does.

*(**ED** puts on make-up.)*

**DOUG.** What's the matter with you Ed?

Don't you ever wanna smile? Laugh? Take a load off?

**ED.** Why don't you *make* me laugh.

Doug?

**DOUG.** Eddie. I know better, okay? I knew you when your hair was floppy, knew you when you covered up your pimples with your Mom's makeup.

**ED.** I still do that.

**DOUG.** Knew you when you used to throw hot dogs into open car windows.

**ED.** I thought you wanted to talk about something.

**DOUG.** I knew you when you used to go the beach and dance around.

**ED.** *(sharp)* Jolly fuck aren't ya?

**DOUG.** Hey. Hey. Hey!

I'm just enjoying the good life you got for me here Ed. What a lucky sonofabitch I am.

What's Brooklyn compared to this? For the past two months I get to bang a drum while some old broad tries to find another clam in her linguine.

*(strong)* Show me how you do the face.

**ED.** What face?

**DOUG.** The face you do, show me how you do it.

**ED.** You mean this face?

> (**ED** *stops putting on make-up and does his "Retard" face.*
>
> *It's crazy looking.*
>
> **DOUG** *cracks up, laughing.*)

**ED.** There's no trick really. I learned how to do this just from watching TV. No biggie.

**DOUG.** *(still kind of laughing)* So I don't have the gift?

**ED.** Didn't say that.

**DOUG.** I don't have the *ability*?

**ED.** You don't have any control.

**DOUG.** So you're saying I shouldn't take a shit on stage tonight.

**ED.** I'm saying: Don't jerk off on it this time.

**DOUG.** I'm serious about this.

**ED.** You couldn't be serious if you were bleeding to death.

**DOUG.** Lola thinks I'm serious.

**ED.** You mean Lola doesn't laugh at your jokes.

**DOUG.** She wants to know why I don't have more to do in the act.

**ED.** Tell her it's cause you're not funny.

**DOUG.** She wants to know why the TV people haven't come up yet.

**ED.** She does, does she?

**DOUG.** What are you proud of Ed?

That the fuckin bears out here know your name?

**ED.** Enough, enough –

**DOUG.** That you're the one with "the bucks the money the status."

**ED.** Status? Status?

You are drunk.

Have you seen where we are? Have you?

Spiders in the shower drains.

Floors smell like a monkey's armpit.

The people here would rather watch vacuum cleaners race than watch us.

**DOUG.** Maybe you should go find a book depository.

Take out your frustrations.

(**DOUG** *mimes Oswald taking aim.*

*He mimes Kennedy waving and then getting his head blown off.*

*He mimes Jackie O. waving, seeking Kennedy and jumping out of the car with blood on her dress.*

*He looks at* **ED.**)

**ED.** Are you being funny now?

**DOUG.** You don't like that?

Cause you're Irish.

**ED.** Cause you're drunk

**DOUG.** Shut up Ed. Shut –

(**DOUG** *throws up on himself.*

*Lights.*

*Music.*

**ED** *puts on his jacket.*

**ED** *is on stage by himself.*

**ED** *does his act for the audience while we see* **DOUG** *clean himself up backstage.*)

**ED.** People tell me I should get married. I'd be happier.

(*Ed talks to someone in the audience.*)

You married?

Look how happy HE is.

(*to someone else*)

You married? I'm very sorry.

(*to someone else*)

You married? Or is this something local?

No no if I got married then I could settle down and die.

My partner Doug got married recently.

He's so happy that every time I see him he asks me to pinch him

He wants to wake up.

My partner tells me that he's worried the spark in the marriage might be gone.

And I can understand.

I come home my girlfriend is Naked. I told her, put on a dress, look sexy!

(*'He waits for laughter'*)

Now allow me to introduce a wonderful young lady who is happily married – sorry guys them's the breaks. If you saw her husband – trust me – you'd know she's a great cook.

I'm not exactly sure what she sees in him but hey, love is blind. Allow me to introduce a woman who I'm sure wants get out here as badly as I do – The lovely Lola!

*(He motions to Lola.* **ED** *watches Lola sing.*

*We hear Lola "sing." We do not see her.*

*Let the music fill the space for a little bit while* **ED** *returns to the dressing room and joins* **DOUG**. **DOUG** *and* **ED** *listen to Lola sing.)*

**DOUG.** She's really good yeah?

**ED.** Yeah.

**DOUG.** Maybe I should hit the drum for her.

**ED.** Couldn't hurt her singing.

**DOUG.** Not very nice.

**ED.** (*serious*) What's she gonna do for you Doug?

**DOUG.** (*joshing*) You want me to draw you a picture?

**ED.** She gonna give you something?

**DOUG.** Not if I keep my pants on.

**ED.** Is she? Really. I'm "serious."

*(Pause)*

**DOUG.** *(suspicious)* Whatta ya doin Ed?

**ED.** She gonna get you on Jack Parr? Ed Sullivan?
She gonna get you off this grimy stage?
Huh?
Doug?
Is she gonna do that for you?

*(**DOUG** hesitates)*

And who could?

**DOUG.** *(sarcastic)* HEY!
I got it!
That's what I got you for!
Right?
You're gonna get me on TV!
Any day now!

**ED.** Yes. Doug. Yes I am.

**DOUG.** Ed. Come on. This is sad. It is. A proud man like yourself acting like a a a

*(**DOUG** makes the retard face.)*

**ED.** *(teaching)* No. No. Doug. We don't do that face anymore.
That's from last summer.
It's old now. We don't like it.

**DOUG.** Who the fuck is We anyway?

**ED.** You know, Me.

*(**DOUG** gets up and goes to his drum.)*

**ED.** *(teasing)* You mad at me now?

*(**DOUG** does a drum roll.)*

**ED.** AH-HA
Dougie is mad.
He wants more to do.

*(Drum roll…)*

**ED.** He's gonna get more to do isn't he?
Dougie's not gonna take it from Ol' Ed anymore.

(*Silence*)

Watch out now, Dougie has a gangster father.

**DOUG.** He's not a gangster.

**ED.** He's got 5 bullet wounds in his back.

**DOUG.** He got those from selling dresses from the back of his car.

(**DOUG** *does a Rim shot.*)

**ED.** Maybe I better be worried. Maybe he gave you a gun.

**DOUG.** The only thing my Dad ever gave me was an old fucking newspaper.

(**DOUG** *does a Rim shot.*)

**ED.** You sure you don't have a gun, Doug?
Might make you're act better.

**DOUG.** For what Ed, why should I need A FUCKING GUN?

**ED.** (*finally explaining, ending the joke*) Maybe then – Doug – you can point it at the audience and *make* em laugh.
Something. Jesus. Something.
I don't wanna be sopping up some old fuck's bread crumbs for the rest of my life,
Your act is shit okay?

(*Pause*)

**DOUG.** So go.

**ED.** Is that a joke?
Me going?

**DOUG.** Yeah. Me and Lola.

**ED.** You and Lola, what?

**DOUG.** She's a good singer.

**ED.** Right.

**DOUG.** Why not?

**ED.** She's gonna have a kid.

**DOUG.** She told you?

**ED.** That's the only thing she's gonna give you, Dougie.

**DOUG.** Fuck you.

> (**ED** *presents* **DOUG** *a fake flower.*)

**ED.** (*a reconciliation*) And this is what *I'm* giving you. So you can remember me.
Take it.
Take it.

> (**DOUG** *puts down his drum sticks and takes the flower.*)

**ED.** It's the least, I mean the very least, I could do.
Now that you're a family man.

> (**DOUG** *puts on the flower.*)

**ED.** Go ahead.
You want more to do.
Let's see what you got.

> *(They stare at each other for a moment and then spotlight on* **DOUG.** *He's on stage by himself.*
>
> *He speaks to the audience.*
>
> *He's got the flower on.*
>
> *He is nervous, bad.)*

**DOUG.** I can tell what you're thinking.
You're wondering if I eat too much.
You've got a point.
Chickens and cows call me Adolph!

> (**DOUG** *speaks to someone in the audience*)

You gonna finish that?
Okay okay.
My left ass cheek gets mail.
Okay.
I'm not saying I'm fat but I've made cereal boxes cry.
Okay, okay, good.

> *(Dead Air. Nothing.)*

Hello? I know you're out there. I can hear you breathing.

*(He pauses and adjusts the flower.)*

You know the lady who gives out the towels at the pool. She's been here a while and she was telling me about her old boyfriends:

Peter, Paul, Matthew.

The man I'm about to introduce.

Ed. He's got a thing for her. He chews her food for her on their dates.

Real Romantic.

*(He goes back to his drum and does a drum roll.)*

And without further ado, it's my pleasure to introduce Steady Eddie from Bayridge!!!

*(**ED** on stage.*

**DOUG** *at the drum.*

**ED** *speaks to the audience.)*

**ED.** Thanks a lot Doug. Thank you.

That was some great great material.

*(**ED** surveys the audience.)*

Doug wasn't born here but he sure did die here.

No his act wasn't that bad and you folks were very nice to him.

It's just in my religion we usually wait a day to bury a guy.

We can't blame Doug for being a little rusty.

It's Very tough for Doug. Very tough.

Just learned to walk upright.

*(**DOUG** hits a Rim shot.)*

No no the truth is he hasn't been sleeping much, he's just become a father.

*(**ED** gives a **DOUG** a round of applause.)*

**DOUG.** Hey I'm used to staying up all night.

**ED.** Me and your wife try to keep it down Doug.

**DOUG.** I know I know but she likes it when you talk dirty.

**ED.** Doug I never talk dirty, you must be confusing me with someone else.

Hey anyone seen the dishwasher?

Ladies and gentlemen you've been a great audience, not for us necessarily…

*(Lights go down.*

**ED** *and* **DOUG** *in the dressing room.*

**ED** *fixes his hair,* **DOUG** *pulls up his pants.*

**ED** *put on a little bit of make-up.*

**DOUG** *looks at a garter of Lola's.)*

**DOUG.** I love Lola. I do. I know I do. She's got these great blue eyes, like a cat.

*(***ED** *is practicing something.)*

**ED.** *(as if he were on TV)* Where am I looking?

Where's the camera? Here?

Ladies and Gentlemen:

Welcome welcome welcome to the Late Night Show.

**DOUG.** But she's got a little bit of hair on her chin.

**ED.** *(still going)* I got the camera now.

Okay, okay.

This is the kinda set you end up on if you don't call your agent for a month.

**DOUG.** But now that she's had a kid she's started to get cellulite on her ass.

**ED.** *(still going)* So without further ado, Here is the one, the only, King of Late Night Television –

**DOUG.** She makes this crazy crazy face when we fuck. It's like –

*(***DOUG** *makes the face of Lola in Bed: Crumpled Forehead, mouth all big, silly noise.)*

**ED.** *(still practicing being on 'TV')* Great to be back, Jack! I love this show. I love the laugh track, the studio audience –

**DOUG.** Could you cut it out?

**ED.** Gotta practice.

**DOUG.** For what?

**ED.** Told you I almost got on Parr yeah?

**DOUG.** (*as if astonished*) What? TV? You did?

**ED.** And I told you that he was gonna send –

(**DOUG** *'snoring.'*)

**ED.** Hysterical.

**DOUG.** (*defending his joke*) Hey that's not so bad.

**ED.** Remember what happened the last time you went out on your own?
Dougie?

**DOUG.** Right.

**ED.** Stick to the fat stuff.
It's what's known as fail-*safe*.

**DOUG.** Safe, Like you.

**ED.** Excuse me?

**DOUG.** Look around. These days the guys that, you know, Go, are guys that say *something*.

**ED.** Some bullshit you mean.

**DOUG.** No, no. They're doing something a little different, that's all.

**ED.** (*really asking him*) You want fucking substance?

**DOUG.** No of course not.

(**DOUG** *puts on a little make-up.*)

**ED.** Something 'real'?
Okay, here, for you:
We got some TV people in the house tonight. For real.

(**DOUG** *takes it in.*)

**DOUG.** Don't worry about me Eddie, don't worry about me at all.
Here, goes. You'll like this. This is some of the good stuff.
The fat stuff.

(**DOUG** *shows his 'new' routine to* **ED**.

*He speaks very deliberately.*)

I like bread.

(**DOUG** *produces a piece of bread.*)

My favorite thing in the world maybe,
other than beer
and shitting
and jerking off
is bread but this          this bread it's
very dry.

**ED.** It's very dry you're right about that.

**DOUG.** So dry
   You getting this Eddie?
   So dry a camel gave me this slice for free.

**ED.** Okay, okay.
   Enough with that Doug

**DOUG.** Right. Enough.
   BIG MAN ED SAYS ENOUGH.
   Must be enough then.

**ED.** You wanna talk about the bread more, go ahead. It's really terrific stuff Doug.
   The TV guys will *Love It*.

**DOUG.** (*aggressive*) This bread is so dry Ed, it's so dry that if you threw it at someone you could kill them.

   (*He throws the bread across the room and makes an explosion noise*)

   BRRRRRREXXXXX

**ED.** That's fascinating.

**DOUG.** Sorry to bore you.

**ED.** (*quick*) Since when?

**DOUG.** I must not have what it takes.

**ED.** Remember what happened the last time you went out on your own.

(**ED** *mimes Doug 'dying' on stage.*)

**DOUG.** Fuck you.

**ED.** Okay, then:
Make me laugh.
Go.

**DOUG.** What?

**ED.** Go ahead. Make me laugh.

(**DOUG** *does something hysterical.*)

**ED.** No no no.

(**DOUG** *goes again.*)

**ED.** (*not good enough*) Come on.

**DOUG.** God I fucking hate you. I do.

**ED.** Very good.

**DOUG.** What do you do?

**ED.** What do *I do*?

**DOUG.** You yes you what do you *do*?

(**ED** *does a funny face.*)

**DOUG.** (*venom*) Show me something new for once!

**ED.** (*a challenge*) New?

**DOUG.** I've heard the tricks
Seen the rabbit.
Come one buddy come on let's see something good.
Now! Right now!

(**ED** *gets in* **DOUG**'s *face.*)

**ED.** Doug?
We gotta work on this.
Doug?
*This* is our Big Night.

(**DOUG** *walks away and starts painting the mirrors of the dressing room with the base make-up.*)

**ED.** (*simmering*) Fuck is that?
Fuck are you *doing*?

**DOUG.** I'm tryin here Ed, I'm tryin.
   You always say, I need to come up with *new* material.
   And I thought tonight
   On our big night
   I might try it out.
**ED.** You're a sad sad man.

   (**DOUG** *draws a big unhappy face on the mirror.*)

**ED.** And fat!

   (*In the mirror* **DOUG** *paints a big stomach under the unhappy face.*)

**ED.** Stop it stop it.
**DOUG.** What else am I?
**ED.** Drunk!
**DOUG.** OH YEAH! Good one!

   (**DOUG** *draws "X"'s over the face's eyes.*)

   Good yeah?
   You like it right, Eddie?

   (*They are almost in hysterics*)

**ED.** I've seen better looking burn victims.

   (**DOUG** *draws the Burns.*
   *More base on the mirror.*
   *Base base base.*
   *They can barely stand.*)

**DOUG.** My hair – look at this – it's gone. GONE!

   (*He streaks the mirror with base.*)

**ED.** Don't do that no more Dougie.
**DOUG.** Or what or what or what
**ED.** (*stone cold dead serious*) I'll fuckin kill you.
**DOUG.** Wow.
**ED.** If you fuck up this tonight I will Doug. Really. Tonight is the night I get the fuck out of the swamp.
   Get dressed. Now.

(**DOUG** *claps his hands once and starts to get dressed quickly. He puts on some make-up.*

*They wait.*

*They pace.*

*They smoke.*

*Nerves.)*

**DOUG.** (*over enthusiastic*) Gonna be great!

**ED.** Hey, I'm not worried.

**DOUG.** Not at all? About Doug the Mug losin it?
   Flippin out?
   Goin a bit a bit batteee?

   (**DOUG** *stares at* **ED.**

   *Hard, like he stole something from him.*)

**ED.** You gonna say something?
   You gonna *do* something?

**DOUG.** (*totally serious*) You think Lola fucks around?

**ED.** Sorry?

**DOUG.** You think Lola   fucks around?

   (**ED** *turns to* **DOUG.**)

**ED.** (*quietly*) You getting into character right now?

   (*The lights go.*

   *The drums go.*

   *The music goes.*

   *Go Go go and go.*

   *It's time for them to go out onstage.*

   **DOUG** *won't let them.*)

**DOUG.** I'm serious.
   Ed I'm serious.

**ED.** (*dismissive*) I know.
   I know you're serious.

**DOUG.** I think she is.

*(The band playing.)*

**ED.** You gonna go out?

Doug?

You gonna go?

Doug?

Are you gonna go?

The TV guys are out there.

Let's go!

*(**DOUG** puts on his big face and goes out.*

*Lights on **DOUG**, he is now onstage.*

*He looks at the audience.*

*Silence. Fear.*

*Silence. Fear.*

*He falls down.*

*He gets up.)*

**DOUG.** Okay, okay.

Good.

*(Pause)*

**DOUG.** Woulda been here sooner but my wife had a friend over.

Nice guy.

He left this suit for me.

*(**ED** on stage, fast.*

*He 'jokes' with **DOUG**.)*

**ED.** Buddy I love your choice in sheets.

**DOUG.** Thanks so much!

Wait till you see my gun.

*(**DOUG** reaches into his pocket and violently pulls out his newspaper.*

*It falls to the ground.*

***ED**, thrown, pauses for a moment.)*

**DOUG.** I forgot it backstage.
Sorry.

(**DOUG** *goes back to his drum.*

**ED** *faces the audience.*)

**ED.** Hey there folks – you gotta excuse him –

(**DOUG** *hits his drum three times very hard and loud.*

**ED** *looks at* **DOUG**, *this is not part of the routine.*)

**ED.** He just learned that. Next week it's the –

(**DOUG** *hits the drum three times very hard and loud.*

**ED** *tries to cover.*)

**ED.** How about that?
Good right?
Next week we're gonna get him the whoppee cushion!

(**ED** *composes himself.*)

Ladies and gentlemen, ladies and gentlemen,
I've heard of rough starts but she said it happens a lot.

(**DOUG** *hits a Rim Shot*)

I've heard of rough starts but usually I get the condom on at least.

*(No Rim Shot)*

I've heard of rough starts but usually they wait till after I'm on stage to throw the tomato.

*(No Rim shot.)*

I've heard of rough starts but this Whaaa????

*(No Rim shot.)*

At least I've got some good help out here.
Right?
Doug?

(**ED** *turns to* **DOUG**.

*Rim Shot*

*Rim Shot*

*Rim Shot*

*Rim Shot)*

We're still practicing.

Next week we're gonna work on walking upright.

It's tough.

Ready, and –

*(The band strikes up over Ed's routine.*

*The lights go down.*

**ED** *and* **DOUG** *in the dressing room.*

*They look at Doug's mirror drawings.*

*A moment.)*

**DOUG.** *(sarcastic)* I think it went really really good.

I think those TV people are gonna be chomping at the bit.

Wow. Just look at em.

*(Pause)*

Ed?

**ED.** I want you to hear me on something, okay?

**DOUG.** *(Like he can't hear him)* What'd ya say?

**ED.** *(quiet)* Are you funny?

**DOUG.** Well, Gee, Boss, I dunno, all I do is hit the drum.

**ED.** *(Livid)* Oh, no.

You do a whole lot more than that Doug, you do oh so much more. Can't you see that?

You are a real real real *talent*.

**DOUG.** Means a lot coming from you.

**ED.** So show me Doug. Show me the great stuff that I've been missing the whole time.

The whole time here the whole goddamm time I'm too thick

I'm too dumb cause I can't see.

I can't see The Brilliant Wonderful Undiscovered Genius right in front of me.

I can't see it cause I'me too busy doing what? –

**DOUG.** You been Suckng up your own air.

**ED.** Right, right, right.

**DOUG.** Parr, Sullivan, TV, all that shit. What is that?

**ED.** *(making a point)* Well Dougie it's *nothing* now.

**DOUG.** Fine.

**ED.** WELL SHOW ME SOMETHING THEN. SHOW ME.

*(**ED** pulls up a chair. Looks to **DOUG**.)*

**DOUG.** Whatta do you want me to do?

**ED.** Let's see the funny stuff. Come on Doug. Come on. Here's your big break. COME ON. Show me now.

**DOUG.** Ed.

**ED.** Fuck you.

I should fucking kill you.

And your kid and your whore wife.

*(**DOUG** hesitates.)*

**DOUG.** Great crowd.

**ED.** Fuck do you want, an intro?

**DOUG.** Could you?

**ED.** *(emphatic)* That's Your Job.

*(**DOUG** takes some breaths. He puts on some make-up.*

*Light on **DOUG**. He is on stage.*

*But he speaks directly to Ed, off stage.)*

**DOUG.** When I was young my mother was a really good looking woman.

Good looking woman. Yeah.

She used to come home and on her skin I could smell this cheap perfume.

She has been out. Carrying on.

My Mom was a party girl so she'd smell like this combo of sherry and perfume. Smell was all over: in her hair, on her ears, her neck, and on this fur coat some guy had bought her.

And when she'd come home – it'd be late – and she'd give me a hug and that perfume-sherry smell would get on me
in my hair on my shirt on my hands on everything.

All over this smell.

Like all over.

*(Now* **DOUG** *talks directly to the audience.)*

And then when I was in bed I'd smell her and I'd start to think of my Mom fucking guys. Giving em blowjobs, in the back of cabs.

In Flop houses.

In Barroom bathrooms.

Her ass on the sink, some guy just – you know – fucking my Mom.

Just fucking her.

And the one time

One time I'm in bed and I her see go the bathroom, and she's just in a shirt, and no underwear.

Saw my Mom's cunt see.

Saw it.

Right there.

I'm lookin at it.

And then

I started

I started to feel

This pressure in my legs

Yeah.

Pressure in my stomach

And I then

I put my hand on my cock.

My little cock.

And everything got all wet.

It was so wet all over the sheets all over the sheets all

over my hand and my stomach and hands and tee-shirt.

(**DOUG** *looks to the audience.*)

What?

You're acting like you *never* jerked off to your Mom before.

(*making it simple*) I told you, my Mom was *really really* pretty.

(*Doug turns to* **ED.**)

There. That's it.

(*Lights down.*)

**ED.** Doug.

**DOUG.** Yeah.

**ED.** That's.

What is that?

(**DOUG** *shrugs*

**DOUG** *and* **ED** *are now in the dressing room.*

**ED** *fixes his hair,* **DOUG** *pulls up his pants.*

**DOUG** *is feeling a bit confident.*)

**DOUG.** I'm gonna get a drink, if you want to come.

**ED.** You *celebrating* something?

**DOUG.** Me? No. Me?

**ED.** You think you're onto something special now?

**DOUG.** You know how Dougie loves his Bourbon.

(**ED** *looks hard at* **DOUG.**)

**ED.** Sure the kid loves it when you get bombed.

**DOUG.** (*As if he forgot*) What kid?

OOOHHH, the kid! No no no, he joins me and we have a drink together.

**ED.** Could you pass the base?

**DOUG.** You gonna do some drawings?

**ED.** Pass the base Doug.

*(**ED** looks at himself in the mirror.)*

I can't believe I'm up here another summer.

*(The spotlight comes up on **DOUG**. Doug on stage.*

*He speaks to the audience.)*

**DOUG.** I wanna tell you all about how I grew up. Yeah, it's something else, it really is.

My father is the one, taught me about women. How to treat em. In the summer he would take me to the Park to look at the girls on their shiny bikes; college girls with short hair and jeans. My Dad called em "dykes" but to me they were just gorgeous: laughing and pulling their shirts up cause their tits were coming out.

One time, one time this one girl with a really tight sweater she was riding her bike down a hill without using her hands just going down going down the hill holding her hands over her head, and I thought she might actually take off.

**ED.** Like this?

*(**ED** tries to 'levitate.'*

**DOUG** *looks at him.)*

**DOUG.** *(back to the routine)* Right, that's great.

And as she rides down the hill my Dad says "I hope she breaks her face"

And I said "hey Dad, that's not nice thing to say to a girl like that"

So he said "you're right"

And he threw a rock at her.

*(Lights down.*

**DOUG** *and* **ED** *in the dressing room.)*

**DOUG.** What about that? What'd ya think? That went well.

*(**ED** puts on the make-up.)*

**DOUG.** You should do some drawings Ed. I'm telling you: You'll feel better.

**ED.** Maybe it'll make me wake up.

(**ED** *takes the make up and writes I HATE YOU on the mirror.*)

**DOUG.** Good stuff Ed.

**ED.** (*getting desperate*) These fucks come up here for the weekend to see a show and you hear them on line in the cafeteria or in the bathroom taking a shit and they just talk talk talk.

They talk about going to night clubs, some chick they banged in the back of a cab, they talk about snorting something, partying.

**DOUG.** Hey I party.

(**DOUG** *toasts*)

**ED.** (*continuing*) And here we are, up here – still still still – looking at squirrels hump each other. Taking naps on couches. Getting rained on.
And for you, well, look:

Lola's not getting any gigs, right?
Your son's what? Two years old now?
It's tough. It's gotta be tough for you.

**DOUG.** You're a real friend Ed, thanks.

**ED.** You're my buddy.

(*Pause*)

**ED.** (*explaining again*) Some of the guys who come up here, some of them know people.

**DOUG.** (*fake enthusiasm*) They do? Like who?

**ED.** They're connected. They talk about what they see.
To people who could get us out of here.

**DOUG.** What're you saying Ed?

**ED.** You know the stuff you've been doing.
You know what I mean.

(*A beat.*)

**DOUG.** You don't like it.

**ED.** Didn't say that. I'm talking about these guys.

**DOUG.** You're saying "Watch it Doug."

   The people who come here they *know* people.

**ED.** You still having a good time up here? Doug? How many years we been doing this?

   You still enjoying it?

**DOUG.** Some people like what I do Ed.

**ED.** They're called children.

**DOUG.** They don't want to hear it, the big shots.

**ED.** That's right. I'm sorry but it's true. They don't.

   Okay?

   (**DOUG** *pulls out his newspaper and holds it front of the zipper on his pants.*

   *There is a bulge behind the paper pointed at* **ED.**)

**DOUG.** (*very serious*) What about you?

   What do you think of it?

   You think it's any good?

**ED.** (*looks at paper*) Is that real?

**DOUG.** What do you think of what I do?

**ED.** Fuck you doing?

**DOUG.** Ed?

**ED.** Put that away please Doug.

   (*Pause*)

**ED.** It's different.

   That's what I think.

   I think it's different.

**DOUG.** Good different or bad different?

**ED.** Fuck do you care?

   (**DOUG** *puts away his paper.*)

**DOUG.** I'm thinking about having another drink?

   You want one?

   (**ED** *fixes his hair,* **DOUG** *pulls up his pants.*)

**ED.** Ladies and Gentlemen Doug the Mug!

*(Lights on.*

**DOUG** *on stage, talking to the audience.*

*He starts.)*

**DOUG.** First time I had sex –

*(***ED** *on stage now too.*

*He also talks to the audience.)*

**ED.** Sex!

*(***DOUG** *looks to* **ED**. *Ed is messing with his routine.)*

**DOUG.** I'm on the beach with my good buddy Eddie.

**ED.** There were girls there too.

**DOUG.** We've got knishes we've got beers.

**ED.** We've *also* got a few girls with us

**DOUG.** From Park Slope. Nice girls.

**ED.** Nice girls?

**DOUG.** They've got these little gold necklaces and great great hair.

**ED.** Not wearing their habits anymore.

**DOUG.** And we,

We wanna look good in front of these girls.

**ED.** Wanna look good!

**DOUG.** So me and Ed start to wrestle with each other. Really going at it.

**ED.** Bang Boom Bing

**DOUG.** And as we're wrestling Ed falls on top of me, knee first, right onto my cock.

**ED.** Where?

**DOUG.** He puts his knee right there.

**ED.** Show me where again!

**DOUG.** It's not funny.

It really really hurt.

I even cried a little bit

**ED.** So did the girls.

**DOUG.** Well this one girl, Amelia.

Irish Italian girl she didn't come all the way out to this part of Brooklyn for nothing.

She wants you know

**ED.** To kiss, get felt up,

**DOUG.** Fingered – at least.

**ED.** At least!

**DOUG.** So we go to my house. Not so far away.

Mom is out.

Brother is in the Army.

No-one is home.

**ED.** (*referring to* **DOUG**) No-one is home.

**DOUG.** And as I'm walking up the stairs with this girl I'm thinking fuck

I can't fuck.

**ED.** It's terrible.

**DOUG.** My dick is totally broken.

But this girl's here and she wants to. This is my first time and she really wants to and fuck and fuck fuck my dick is like

Snapped.

**ED.** Snapped!

**DOUG.** So we're under the sheets and she starts.

She's Laying there. Naked. She wants me to.

So I start to try. I try and try and try.

**ED.** (*overlapping with Doug*) Try and try and try try try –

**DOUG.** I'm pushing my hips into her and my dick is sliding around and to the side and under her ass and over her you know

over her and I could feel she wants to.

She really does it's like she's like waiting for me.

Made me so crazy.

She tries to guide     me          get a handle on it but it's broken I can't tell her that but it's true it's broken.

I came real quick.

Total disaster.

**ED.** Like this show?

(**DOUG** *turns to* **ED.**)

**DOUG.** My buddy Eddie – he really fucked me.

(**DOUG** *walks behind the curtain.*

**ED** *still on stage.*)

**ED.** (*he's wrapping up the show*) Hey Dougie could you speak a little slower next time, the people here are trying to sleep.

I want to thank you all for coming out tonight.

If case of nuclear disaster just come back here – we'll be here. We will. Place is about as funny as a shelter. Thanks a lot.

(**ED** *follows* **DOUG** *behind the curtain.*

*An empty stage.*

**DOUG** *comes back out.*

**ED** *comes back out.*

**DOUG** *disappears.*

**ED** *disappears.*

**DOUG** *comes out threateningly holding a newspaper with a bulge behind it and pointing it at the audience.*

**ED**, *concerned, runs out on stage after him and guides him off.*

**DOUG** *walks off.*

**ED** *walks off.*

*The empty stage.*

*The curtain opens to reveal…*

**DOUG** *and* **ED** *in the dressing room.*

*It's a mess.*

*Bottles and clothes strewn about.*

*Silence)*

**DOUG.** (*pissed*) I just saw a shooting star.
**ED.** What?
**DOUG.** (*bad pun*) I'm looking at one right now.
  Here one day then the next          Gone.
**ED.** (*tight lipped*) Yeah, that's me.
  *(Pause)*
**DOUG.** Talk to me Ed.
  What's going on?
**ED.** Okay, let's talk. Yeah.
**DOUG.** You could say something to me.
**ED.** Yeah?
**DOUG.** You could say – "Hey fuck you pal"
**ED.** Okay.
**DOUG.** You could say "You're fuckin up our lives man"
**ED.** I've done enough already tonight.
**DOUG.** Have you?
**ED.** I've shown you enough.
**DOUG.** Is that what you've been doing?
  Showing me? Is that what that was?
**ED.** You're asking me?
**DOUG.** Can I? Am I allowed?
**ED.** No. No you're not.
  You're not allowed to ask me anything.
**DOUG.** I see what's going on here.
**ED.** I doubt that.
**DOUG.** Well.
  I used to introduce you.
**ED.** (*DUH*) Ah, But Times have changed, haven't they!
  Now I'm the guy who warms up.
**DOUG.** I always did want to make a name for myself.
**ED.** Yes. They certainly are talking about you. They can't shut up about it.
**DOUG.** That's what we wanted isn't it Eddie?
  Ed?

**ED.** And what do you *think* they're saying?

**DOUG.** "That guy he's he's… "

**ED.** Which guy are they talking about?

**DOUG.** Me.

**ED.** Yes they're talking about you.

**DOUG.** "He's the best"

**ED.** Yeah right.

Isn't that obvious by how many laughs you get?

**DOUG.** Laughs aren't everything, Ed.

**ED.** *(looking at Doug)* Fuck you.

Fuck you.

I fucking hate you.

**DOUG.** You could do better than that Eddie.

No?

**ED.** No. Not me.

I'm pretty *easy*.

**DOUG.** *(hurt)* Well then, tonight when you go out you should do some of the really funny stuff!

That stuff that always kills!

The classic material!

Make some faces.

Do some old puns about the wife.

**ED.** Right.

**DOUG.** Or maybe you could do something really hip: put on black face and dance around.

(**ED** *considers*)

Hey, Ed. You could do a bit about where you make fun of the screaming little girl whose skin is getting burned off with napalm.

(**DOUG** *does a bit of the screaming Napalm Girl.*)

That seems about right for you.

**ED.** Right. Easy.

Here.

Before I go.

(**ED** *gives* **DOUG** *Lola's garter.*)

**DOUG.** What's this?

**ED.** Lola's.

**DOUG.** She leave this at your cabin?

**ED.** Yeah she did.

**DOUG.** (*playing along*) Cause you two were getting steamy.

(*Pause*)

**ED.** (*not playing*) She left em at my cabin.

**DOUG.** That's good.
Why?

**ED.** Why?
Why?

(**ED** *laughing*)

Oh you are good my friend you are good

I'm gonna get on now.

(**ED** *leaves to go on.*)

**DOUG.** Ed.
Ed.
Jesus fuck.
Fuck.
Ed. Ed. Ed.

(**ED** *comes back in*)

**ED.** (*head of steam*) Your Fuckinwife comes to me.
She's crying
She's crying Doug I hate it I hate when she cries.

**DOUG.** Happen a lot?

**ED.** It does. But you're too busy getting drunk and talking about your broken dick to even give a shit.

**DOUG.** (*sarcastic*) Well thanks for looking out for her Ed, how's she feeling.

**ED.** We talk.

**DOUG.** Talk?
You're a sad man.
You gotta go try and fuck my wife.

**ED.** Hey hey hey.

**DOUG.** Fuck is wrong with you.
Giving me this?

**ED.** Just trying to get your attention.

**DOUG.** Okay you got it.

**ED.** What are you doing?

**DOUG.** Who are you again?

**ED.** I'm your partner.

**DOUG.** You're not funny.

*(**ED** does the 'retard' face.)*

**DOUG.** That face isn't funny. It's old. You taught me that.

**ED.** What about this face?

*(**ED** makes the face of Lola in Bed. Crumpled Forehead, mouth all big, silly noise.)*

See how I'm crinkling up my forehead, does that look familiar to you?

*(**DOUG** takes a swing at **ED**.)*

**ED.** That was a joke.

*(Lights and Sound and*
*Music and go and go and go.)*

**DOUG.** Don't you have to get out there?
Warm up the crowd?

**ED.** Fat fuck.

**DOUG.** Oh Fat! Bing!

**ED.** Boing!

*(**DOUG** sits down to watch **ED**.)*

**DOUG.** Off you go.
You hack.

*(Spotlight on **ED** on stage.*
*He talking to the audience.*
***ED** is super smug, cool.*
*This is his new 'act'.)*

**ED.** I can't believe I'm still here, doing this act.
   I know     neither can you.

   *(Funny voice)*

   "It's killin me already"

   *(He looks at the audience.)*

   Am I Right? Am I right?

   *(He smiles A Shit Eating Smile.)*

   What's like the worst thing you could do to a guy?
   Take his job?
   Take his wife?
   Guy in front here, he's grinning.
   "No no, please don't take the wife"

   *(referring to a laugh)*

   Thanks for that.
   What did you come for? Revenge?
   If there were some Indians here I could trade em for a laugh.

   *(Waits for a laugh)*

   That joke hasn't worked since Japan and Germany had a chance.
   Back when we fought real wars now it's like are we fighting the Commies or is it a rock concert?

   *(He point at someone in the audience.)*

   This hippie here he knows what I'm taking about.
   All the ladies here are very jealous of this guy's hair.

   *(to the same guy)*

   You need a hair cut call me. I know a guy. He's great, used to work in the circus.
   I tell you, these hippies today, it's not that they're dirty, it just they think we're being invaded when they hear foreign words, you know, like soap.
   I'm just kidding about the hippies:
   I know they got soap on Park Avenue.

Am I right? Am I right?

*(He takes it in.)*

Okay, folks, let's cut to the chase.
The man you've been waiting for.
And don't say I didn't warn you.
Please give it up for my partner Doug the Mug.
That guy is hard to miss, I tell ya
Here we go.

*(**DOUG** enters the stage.*

**DOUG** *and* **ED** *are on stage together.*

**DOUG** *turns to* **ED**.*)*

**DOUG.** Thanks Ed thanks a lot. Thanks.
Really cutting edge there.
Going after hippies like that – you wearing a wire man?
Jesus.

*(Pause*

**DOUG** *turns out to the audience.)*

Anyone seen my wife?

*(He turns back to* **ED**.*)*

Ed?
Where'd you drop her off tonight?

**ED.** I'm sure she's just back there helping out the dishwashers.

**DOUG.** Right, right.
So how do feel right now Eddie.
How do you feel?
Feel good, man?

**ED.** Feel good, Doug.

**DOUG.** Our big show, right?

**ED.** Not if you include the audience.

**DOUG.** *(to the audience)* You know Ed told me that tonight we have some big wigs in the house.
I don't see any big wigs.

Ed do you?
You see any important people out here.
Anyone?

(**DOUG** *really looks.*

**DOUG** *points to someone in the audience.*)

HEY!
This guy a big wig I think.

(**DOUG** *stares at the same person in the audience.*)

Ed when you said there were *connected* people here I didn't know you meant they were like *connected*. Connected to a gun.
This guy here is just like my father.
Dad wasn't around much, so I just called him Willie.
And Willie was a mobster.
You don't know anything about that right Mister?
But those are some *nice* rings you've got on.
Where'd you get those rings?

*(as if he heard the answer)*

Some dead fuck in Jersey?
Charming fucking guys these mobsters are. Really.

When my brother got killed in the War my father Willy sent me and my Mom a TV.
And you know what?
We almost totally forgot about my brother. That TV!
I tell ya. I can't even remember my brother's name anymore.

We kept the door of his room closed and cause of the TV and all that laughing from the Ed Sullivan show You wouldn't even notice the closed door.
You wouldn't think about what was on the other side.
You wouldn't think about your brother and his blown off head.
I guess wise guys are used to that kinda thing.
Give each other a lot of television sets.

(**DOUG** *looks back to the same spot in the audience.*)
Yeah?
That right?
Like if you got wacked would the boys chip in and get your wife –
(*scolding*) that is your wife isn't it?
I wonder what it's like to break a man's knees. Or his thumbs.
(*Back to the same person in the audience*)
This guy's looking at me, he's thinking,
"buddy you're gonna find out soon enough'
(*Silence*)
You got something you wanna say to me pal?
(**DOUG** *stares at the person in the audience.*

*He seems as if he is about to attack the audience member.*

**ED** *comes out on stage and stands in front of* **DOUG**.)

**ED.** Thanks very much for coming out tonight.
Thanks very much.

(*The band strikes up.*

**DOUG** *and* **ED** *in the Dressing Room.*

*It's been totally destroyed.*

*Two empty glasses on the table.*)

**ED.** (*somber, soft, determined*) Was downstairs earlier. You know.
With our manager. He wanted to talk to me.
**DOUG.** That guy can speak?
**ED.** Our Manager's a little pissed off.
**DOUG.**(*impersonating their manager, a dumb thug*)
"Whasswit the routineee felaaaahhs?
Wasswiththeroutineeee?
Jokes. Yuh gots ta make jokes."

**ED.** (*enjoying it*) Yes, that's very good.

**DOUG.** "Whasswitttdatheroutine?"

**ED.** (*Joining the fun*) "You gots ta knows whats dese people likes"

**DOUG.** That guy is a savage.

**ED.** (*still impersonating*) "Yas gots da do duh jokes uh else dem folks is gonna spilt lickity split."

**DOUG.** They're not gonna split Ed.

**ED.** "And if dey splits den we's gots probuulemss, ya unastand, probuulms, an youse don wan probuulemsss do ya?"

**DOUG.** What's he gonna do?

Fire us?

Beat us to death with hoola-hoops.

**ED.** "Probuulems"

**DOUG.** You're trying to scare me.

**ED.** Both of us

Need to get back to it.

Or else.

You know?

**DOUG.** Right sure.

**ED.** You wanna go back to Brooklyn and sell dresses out of the back of a car? That what you want? You want to become a fucking stenographer? A shoe-saleman? You wanna be famous as they guy who makes the best Martini on Avenue U?

(**DOUG** *looks for a drink.*)

**DOUG.** Those fucks took my whiskey.

**ED.** Dougie.

You can't do this anymore.

**DOUG.** It looks like Watts in here.

**ED.** You should take a break.

**DOUG.** Where am I gonna go?

The caves?

**ED.** You and Lola could go somewhere.

**DOUG.** That's a great fucking idea Ed!

We'll elope.

Go to an Island.

Kick back and live off our money and our love.

**ED.** Okay, okay

**DOUG.** We're staying.

**ED.** Okay then –

If you wanna stay here,

We gotta get back to it.

Right?

**DOUG.** (*manager again*) "Jokes, ya gots to make jokes"

**ED.** Come on Doug.

The funny stuff.

Let's go.

Go.

Make me laugh

**DOUG.** I can't.

**ED.** Go.

Now.

**DOUG.** No

**ED.** GO

(**DOUG** *decides to practice with* **ED.**

*This goes at a furious pace.*)

**DOUG.** Here there buddy ya ever seen this walk

(**DOUG** *does a Funny walk.*)

**ED.** No

**DOUG.** How about this?

(**DOUG** *does a Funny voice.*)

**ED.** No

**DOUG.** (*Super-harsh*) Come on Ed.

**ED.** Go

**DOUG.** Fine Ed fine.

Whah whah whah whah whah blah blah blah blah.

There? Fuckin there?

**ED.** Let's see it

**DOUG.** Fine here.

*(**DOUG** puts on the 'retard' face.)*

Hey there buddy. Hey there, how are ya? How are ya?

**ED.** Yes! There is it! That's what we gotta have now!

**DOUG.** Whaatta ya know about this:

I don't want to say I'm fat but

I don't want to say I'm fat but

I walked into a restaurant the other day and the menus hid under the table.

I don't want to say I'm fat but I use mashed potatoes for deodorant.

I don't want to say I'm fat but in the winter the Eskimos throw spears at me.

I don't want to say

I don't want to say

*(breaking)*

I can't do it.

I can't do it Ed.

**ED.** You're disgusting you know that.

**DOUG.** Okay, okay, okay here I go.

I don't wanna say I'm fat but when my kid said he wanted to use the car he put they keys in my ass
Okay enough enough.

**ED.** No. It's not. Keep going

**DOUG.** No Ed.

**ED.** Try harder fatman. Try harder.

**DOUG.** Show me.

**ED.** You can do better.

**DOUG.** I am better ya idiot. I am.

That's why she married me.

*(A beat.)*

**ED.** Right.

*(DOUG and ED start to get ready for their next act.*

*ED fixes his hair, DOUG pulls up his pants.)*

**DOUG.** Don't get too upset or nothing now Eddie.

**ED.** Just try not to actually kill someone on stage tonight.

**DOUG.** Thought you liked that stuff.

**ED.** Cocksucker.

**DOUG.** Fuck you.

**ED.** Your mother.

*(DOUG takes a big drink.*

*Drum Roll.*

*Lights*

*Lights*

*Lights*

*Music*

*Music*

*And... )*

**VOICE OVER.** *LADIES AND GENTELMEN, INTRODUCING THE FUNNIEST COUPLE SINCE NIXON AND AGNEW, A WONDERFUL DUO, DOUG THE MUG AND HIS BEAUTIFUL WIFE, LOLA!!!!!*

*(For this next act Doug plays Lola and Ed plays Doug. The lines that say "Doug" should be read by the actor playing Ed, and the lines that say "Lola" should be read by the actor playing Doug. They can use their dressing room as a 'set.)*

*(Lola comes out on stage.)*

**LOLA.** *(Shrill, angry, mean)* Dougie, Dougie where are ya? Where are ya Dougie???

*(She looks around.*

*She looks around.*

*'Doug' appears. He's 'drunk')*

**DOUG.** (*a ham*) Baby I was just cixing the fabinet.

**LOLA.** You're drunk!

**DOUG.** Shotz aaaallll around.

**LOLA.** (*low and guttural*) I'm gonna leave you if you keep this up.

**DOUG.** (*light and big*) Promise?

**LOLA.** Watch me.

**DOUG.** Wait, wait. Let's dance.

*('Doug' gets 'friendly.' They dance.)*

**LOLA.** Get off!

**DOUG.** I'm tryin, stay still.

*('Doug' puts on his Big Shit Eating Grin.)*

**DOUG.** Am I right? Am I right?

**LOLA.** I'll wallop ya

**DOUG.** Kinky!

**LOLA.** GET THE HELLOFFAHME!

*(They gather themselves.*

*'Doug' goes to 'read' in the chair. Very distinguished.)*

**LOLA.** That's better. Now I can practice my singing.

*(Lola 'sings' for a moment.)*

**DOUG.** Lookat that!

**LOLA.** What.

**DOUG.** The dogs came back. They're singing too.

*('Doug' howls.)*

**LOLA.** Ima good singah Dougie!

**DOUG.** And I'm a good comedian.

*(He turns out to the audience, once again wearing his big Shit-Eating Grin Face.)*

**DOUG.** Am I Right? Am I Right?

**LOLA.** You never appreciate me. What I do.

**DOUG.** *(hasn't heard her)* What'd ya say?

**LOLA.** You never app – .

*('Doug' is 'snoring')*

**LOLA.** Wake up!

*(She wallops him. Hard)*

**DOUG.** Wow Lola ya really got a lotta power there.

**LOLA.** Well I'm pissed off.

*(Lola wallops him again. Really hard. Way Too hard.)*

**LOLA.** Whore-Monger.

*('Doug' pause he takes stock of the situation.)*

**DOUG.** What about you baby?
Even the trees have been getting some from you. I come home and there's pinecones on my pillow.

**LOLA.** Trees stay hard!

**DOUG.** You better watch it.

**LOLA.** HA!

**DOUG.** That funny to you?

**LOLA.** First time you've made me laugh in years.

*(Their masks start to fall away. We hear their real voices.)*

**DOUG.** What do you know about comedy?

**LOLA.** More than you you hack.

**DOUG.** Hack?

*('Doug' does a stupid face.)*

**LOLA.** *(not even joking at all)* I hate that face
It makes me sick.
I'm tired of looking at that stupid dumb face of yours.

**DOUG.** *(also not joking)* Stop it right now!

**LOLA.** Or what?
Whatta ya gonna do Dougie?
Leave me?

*("Doug" covers his eyes.)*

**DOUG.** (*melodramatic*) Please Don't leave me. Please. God, I couldn't stand. It

(*to audience*)

She gone yet?

(*Lola comes back with a baby stroller.*

*'Doug' sees the stroller.*)

**DOUG.** Look who it is! The apple of my eye!

(*Lola picks up a baby who waves to 'Doug'.*

*Doug is not amused by this at all.*

*We should believe that there is a real baby on stage.*)

**LOLA.** Say good-bye to your Daddy.

**DOUG.** Looks just like me.

(*breaking*)

What are you doing?

**LOLA.** Yeah, he does. Looks just like his Daddy.

(*She holds up the kid and looks at him then at 'Doug'*

*She puts the baby back in the carriage.*)

**LOLA.** He's got a lot in common with him too.

(*She pours some booze in the carriage.*)

**DOUG.** (*not joking anymore, genuinely concerned*) Okay, okay, Lola,

Lola,

Lola

that's enough.

You'll make the kid upset.

(*Crying.*

*Pause.*

*Weirdness.*)

**LOLA.** Kid's fucking freezing, I'm gotta warm him up.

(*She exits with stroller.*

**ED** *drops his 'Doug' mask. He's not playing any more.*)

**ED.** (*rattled*) Well thanks a lot ladies and gentleman. My wife, my partner, my wife, well you know what I'm saying. She tends to get a little upset when we fight. No biggie. I got fifty bucks. She'll be back.

(*A burning crib rolls onto stage.*

**ED** *runs to the crib, tries to put out the fire.*)

**ED.** Hey

Hey

Hey. Jesus.

Hey!

Could I get some fucking help here please?

HEY!

Jesus. Come on.

Could I.

Could I.

Help!

(*The real* **DOUG** *comes on stage holding the kid.*)

**DOUG.** Eddie!

A little trust how bout

Huh?

Think I'd do that to my kid?

(*They watch the crib burn.*

*The curtain falls.*

**DOUG** *and* **ED** *come on in front of the curtain.*

**ED** *is taking off all his make-up. He does this violently.*

**DOUG** *watches him a little bit.*)

**DOUG.** I really had you there, huh?

**ED.** Lola musta loved it.

**DOUG.** (*like he doesn't know*) Who's Lola?

OHHHH, right, Lola.

She loved it. Loved it.

**ED.** Right, right.

**DOUG.** Took the kid and split. Had to spread the word I guess.

*(Silence.*

**ED** *takes off make-up)*

**DOUG.** You like it?
The new stuff.

**ED.** Was it funny?

**DOUG.** You wouldn't know funny.

**ED.** You don't put your kid –

**DOUG.** Hey.
Not my kid.

**ED.** How the fuck do you know, you maniac.

*(**ED** continues to take off his make up.)*

**DOUG.** Let 'em fire us!

**ED.** Yeah let 'em.

**DOUG.** Yeah let 'em

*(He takes out the fake flower. It squirts water.)*

**DOUG.** Lookatthis. Coulda used it tonight.
Get it?

**ED.** Fuck you Kike.

**DOUG.** *(taking that in)* Ed. That's unnecessary.

**ED.** Did you see our manager?

**DOUG.** "Whatswiththefunnystuff"

**ED.** Did you see his face?
Did you those guys with him?

**DOUG.** Don't worry: I'm gonna put on the flower.

**ED.** No.
I need it.

**DOUG.** *(referring to flower)* This?

**ED.** Yes. That.
That. Yes.

**DOUG.** I don't think so Boss.

**ED.** *(simple)* It's mine. I gave it to you.

**DOUG.** And you don't wanna share?

**ED.** Gimmie the Flower.

Okay?

(**DOUG** *takes off flower gives it back to* **ED.**)

**DOUG.** (*as if it's all fine*) Well at least I got my lady.

**ED.** Right.

**DOUG.** Got my kid.

**ED.** Yup.

(*Pause*)

**ED.** You got your routine.

**DOUG.** Right.

**ED.** The good stuff, right Dougie?

**DOUG.** Right.

**ED.** There you go then. It's what you wanted.

**DOUG.** Okay then. Great.

**ED.** Okay.

**DOUG.** (*breaking*) Ed she really left, she really did.

**ED.** I know she did Doug. I know it.

**DOUG.** I don't know what to do.

**ED.** Well.

**DOUG.** I really don't know what to do.

I feel sick.

**ED.** I gottta take a walk.

**DOUG.** Ed.

**ED.** I gotta get some air.

**DOUG.** They got plenty of that up here.

**ED.** Stop it.

(*Pause*)

**ED.** What?

**DOUG.** Nothing. Nothing at all.

**ED.** Some of the TV guys want to talk.

To me.

They liked when I made fun of the hippies.

**DOUG.** Right.
Really?

**ED.** Doug. Leave it. Kay? Just Leave it.

*(A beat.*

**ED** *leaves.*

**DOUG** *sits on stage alone.*

**DOUG** *pulls up his pants.*

*He addresses the audience.)*

**DOUG.** It wasn't always this good for me.

I used to have a family.

Wheeeew.

Used to have a wife and a kid.
I used to have a son.

Wheeeww.

Glad I got rid of that.

I mean – that shit was the worst. The absolute worst.
You wanna know how bad it was?

Me and the wife used to go to the lake where it was very very sunny.

And she can't swim so she'd sit next to me and paint her toenails purple and I'd lie down and the boy would climb on top of me. He was really heavy and he'd climb up around my head and put his little hands on my ears, breathe on my neck.

I could like feel his little body right next to mine.

Let me tell you, I'm glad that shit is over.

That was real hell.

Who the fuck wants that?

Now it's just great for me

Look at what I got.

Look at all this I got.

Just look at it.

Nice, right?

You wanna trade with me?

No?

Come on. Come on.

Okay, last chance.

This is your last chance.

I got a great offer from a bear who wants this whole space.

He offered me a jar of honey.

No lie.

He did.

(**ED** *walks onto stage in a fancy winter coat and a new haircut.*

**DOUG** *notices* **ED** *and turns to him.*

*It's been a while.*)

**DOUG.** How was that? You like that? I felt I was really really you know like

onto something man

like     I was onto something.

I did.

**ED.** Wasn't bad.

**DOUG.** You think?

**ED.** Didn't you hear the laughs?

**DOUG.** I musta missed them.

**ED.** Laughs aren't everything.

**DOUG.** That what they taught you on 'The Tonight Show'?

**ED.** Those guys taught me how to stand still. For the camera.

**DOUG.** Oh yeah?

**ED.** Here we can move around all we want.

**DOUG.** We?

    Fuckin we?

**ED.** You.

    You can talk in funny voices

**DOUG.** (*funny voice*) "whatta ya mean?"

**ED.** The TV guys don't go for that crazy stuff so much.
**DOUG.** They have class, right?

*(Pause)*

**ED.** Doug.

Look.

You can do better than this.

You're Doug the mug.
**DOUG.** (*angry*) And who the fuck are you again?
**ED.** Aw, shucks, you know me.

I'm the guy on TV
**DOUG.** (*super-resentful*) Oh! Yes, yes, on TV!

You're the guy on TV!

I knew I recognized you from somewhere!
**ED.** (*that's right*) You recognize this?

*(**ED** launches into his TV routine.)*

"Hey there folks

So glad to be here tonight.

Oh wait.

Where's the camera?

*(It's the same bit:* **ED** *"looks and points at the imaginary camera.")*

Oh, hey there America."
**DOUG.** Very good very good
**ED.** (*continuing*) "Hello and welcome to our show.

Now we've got a special treat for you tonight.

A blast from the past, if you will.

*('scolding')*

Your parents are here and they want to know what you're doing with your life.

No no no.

Tonight, there's a special guy, a guy who I think you always wanted to see,

> He's been doing comedy for a while now
> James Madison was a big fan.
> Welcome,
> Doug the Mug."

*(He looks to **DOUG**. **DOUG** doesn't move.)*

**ED.** And then there's applause…

**DOUG.** Yeah.

**ED.** Applause and you get up.
   You get up.

**DOUG.** I get up.

**ED.** You get up.

**DOUG.** I don't move around so well these days. My legs never really healed, our manager's "friends"…

**ED.** I could use someone like that.
   In my act.

**DOUG.** I got lots of offers Ed.

**ED.** Seriously Doug, My monkey is sick, I could use you.

**DOUG.** Well you know I'd love to but later tonight I gotta a gig by the creek.

**ED.** Doug, I'm trying.

**DOUG.** I forgot what a good pal you are to me.

**ED.** *(a real offer)* If you want, we could go to The City and

**DOUG.** Get Famous?

**ED.** I am Famous.

**DOUG.** I could talk about how my fingers get frostbitten. How the green green land here isn't green anymore, it's grey.

**ED.** They got nice warm lights in the Studio. And the ushers bring you whiskey if you ask them.

**DOUG.** I could talk about how the pipes get frozen in the bathroom during the winter so I gotta take a shit in the ground. How sometimes I use leaves for toilet paper, how I can't really feel my fingers, my nose, how the snow gets into my socks.

I got great great stuff about frostbitten fingers, about cold noses, about frozen pipes.

The material here – it's endless.

*(Long Pause.)*

**ED.** Look, you had your shot.

**DOUG.** When was that?

**ED.** When you tried to burn the place down.

**DOUG.** Well. Yeah.

**ED.** So get the fuck up. Come on. Fat piece of shit.
Show me what I've been missing.
What we've all been missing.
Show me.

**DOUG.** Don't start right now.

**ED.** Come on Doug.
For Eddie.

**DOUG.** Who the fuck is Eddie?

**ED.** You know.

Your partner.

**DOUG.** Where?

**ED.** Right here. Now.

**DOUG.** No.

**ED.** You can't do it anymore.

**DOUG.** *You* can't do it anymore.

**ED.** Well. Carson disagrees.

**DOUG.** You're a *fucking* warm up act.

**ED.** At least you're not bitter.

**DOUG.** (*a decision*) Okay. Fine.
I'm gonna answer the bell.

**ED.** DING!

**DOUG.** I'm gonna knock em dead!

**ED.** BANG!

**DOUG.** Here I go.

(**DOUG** *stands up. He slowly walks over to* **ED**. *He does not move so well these days.*

*They look out at the audience.)*

**ED.** You hear that applause? Jesus.
Jesus.
It's thunderous.

*(They're back.)*

Here we go, here we go.
Now wait, where's the camera.
AH-HA!

**(EDDIE** *'finds the camera')*

Hello there welcome welcome welcome to this evening's show.
Before I bring out the Big Guy I wanna introduce my buddy here –

**DOUG.** Hey buddy we just met!

**ED.** Bang!

**DOUG.** Boom!

**ED.** Your kingdom for a cupcake right now.

**DOUG.** You wanna know how fat I am?
I'm so fat.
I am so Fat.

*(Pause as Dougie thinks of it.)*

I'm so fat that this show is gonna be on three stations.

**ED.** *(pleased)* Classic material.

**(DOUG** *launches into a 'classic' routine.)*

**DOUG.** This guy got so close to my wife they asked me to leave for our anniversary.

**ED.** Good good .

**DOUG.** He spends so much time with my son that whenever my kid sees a van he thinks Ed is coming over.

**ED.** Good good.
Here we go here we go.

**DOUG.** I don't wanna say he fucked me over but after he left I sure had lotta stains on my sheets.

**ED.** Can't curse on TV.
We'll edit that out.

Okay?
Doug, okay?

**ED.** Let's give a hand to my partner, Doug the Mug ladies and Gentleman.

*(**DOUG** goes and sits down at his drum.*

**ED** *faces out the audience.)*

**ED.** Next week, we're actually gonna put film in the camera.

*(**ED** finds the camera.)*

Okay okay folks here we go.

Don't worry this won't hurt one bit.

*(**ED** does his Big Shit Eating Grin.)*

Am I Right? Am I Right?

Doug,
Could I get a little help here?

*(**DOUG** hits a Rim shot.)*

**ED.** Thanks very much Doug thanks very much.
Now I didn't always have such a sweet gig here on this show.

Introducing the Big Fella.

No no no

I used introduce someone much Bigger – Doug!

*(Rim shot.)*

I Used to be obscure. A no – body
Like –

*(He 'secretly' points at **DOUG**.)*

Now? Well now I'm famous.

How famous am I?

I'm so famous I was late to this show cause I had to screw a model on a pile of cash.

*(Rim shot.*

*They're starting to roll.)*

**ED.** My partner and I – our old routine wasn't so good. And I'm not gonna say Doug here was extra baggage but I replaced him with a backpack.

*(Rim shot.)*

**ED.** Cause Dougie here, let's just say he wasn't so cut out for it.
He's a little, you know –

*(**ED** makes the 'retard' face*

*Rim shot.)*

That face always kills it does.
That's the face the president made when he found out he forgot to burn those tapes!

*(Rim shot.)*

That's the face those kids made when they found out it wasn't the 'good' kind of acid!

*(Rim shot.)*

My partner taught me that face he did. Didn't you Dougie?

*(Rim shot.)*

That's Dougie at breakfast
After he puts some cornflakes in his Gimlet!

*(Rim shot.)*

I know I know
It's a bad face
A bad face
I shouldn't do it.
But… .

*(**ED** can't resist*

*Makes the face.)*

*Rim shot.)*

I mean That's the face my partner makes when I go visit his wife.

*(No Rim shot)*

And you should see the face she makes!

*(No Rim shot.)*

Hey Doug could I get a rim shot please.
Hey Doug.
Doug?

*(DOUG at his drum. He looks at ED.)*

**DOUG.** That face isn't funny. Even when it's on TV.

**ED.** Doug likes the 'real' stuff. He's one of these hip guys. You can tell from how he smells.

**DOUG.** Stop.
Stop.

**ED.** Hey pal it's just a routine.

**DOUG.** you think I'm just gonna sit there on this stage…

**ED.** *(mocking)* While you make jokes about me?

**DOUG.** And I just take it?

**ED.** You're no kid

**DOUG.** Just cause we're on TV.

**ED.** Thousands of white screens.

**DOUG.** Why'd you come back?

**ED.** Lola wanted to make sure you were okay.
She gets worried and feels guilty sometimes.
I told her it was your choice.

**DOUG.** Bullshit.

**ED.** We got a nice little house now. When you're ready to leave the caves up here you should come visit us. We got some real nice whiskey

**DOUG.** Why'd you come back Ed?

**ED.** Cause I wanted to see what happened to you – Doug the Mug.
Just take a look.

After all that. How "great" you were.

How true?

How real?

No one remembers who you are, not even your kid.

All you are is a rumor. A whisper. A cautionary tale.

**DOUG.** I always did want to be Famous.

**ED.** Bullshit. That's fucking bullshit.

This is not what we wanted. Not at all.

Not at all.

**DOUG.** And What was it that *we* wanted?

**ED.** To do this together.

Doug?

Am I right?

(**ED** *puts on the Big Shit Eating Grin.*)

Am I right? Am I right?

**DOUG.** I wash dishes now, Ed. I'm the dishwasher.

**ED.** I should tell Lola. Maybe she'll come back to you.

**DOUG.** Here's the great part Ed. They got a TV at the Bar. I can watch you Eddie, I can see you on the TV.

**ED.** You tell everyone how I *used* to be.

When I was young.

What fun we used to have.

**DOUG.** (*'drunk'*) Thass my partner –

**ED.** Where'd he gah?

**DOUG.** It's very funny.

**ED.** Me?

**DOUG.** The new guys, *they're* funny.

**ED.** Well they sound a lot like this big fat fuck I used to know.

Who used to tell stories about his Mom.

**DOUG.** Well. Yeah.

**ED.** And how's that for you?

How's that feel to watch them?

**DOUG.** I can't say I like it very much Ed.

**ED.** So you're just gonna let them Take it from you.
Just like that.
You're just going to give up
**DOUG.** What am I gonna do? Take it back?
**ED.** Don't you wanna see your fucking son you selfish fuck?
Your wife?
Me? Huh?
Are you too good for all of it?
Jesus Doug, I need you up there.
I mean *who is* gonna make the fat jokes?

(**DOUG** *pulls out a newspaper. Points it at* **ED.**)

**DOUG.** Don't call me fat any more.
**ED.** Is that a joke?
**DOUG.** You know who used to always call me fat?
**ED.** Who?
**DOUG.** My father, Willie.
**ED.** (*looking at the newspaper 'gun'*) Is that real Doug?
**DOUG.** You know what happened to my father?
**ED.** Can we cut the jokes?
For a fucking second?
Can we do that?
**DOUG.** He gave me a newspaper. He did.

(**DOUG** *unfolds the newspaper.*)

(*a bit forceful*) This one is all about us. All about the duo from Brooklyn.
Shall I read it to you?
Here goes:

"Two comedians, Doug and Ed, also known as Doug the Mug and Steady Eddie from Bayridge were found dead in the Catskills."

Cause of death?
**ED.** No laughs?

**DOUG.** Very good Ed no laughs is what killed us.

**ED.** Kay fine.

(**DOUG** *gives* **ED** *the newspaper.*)

**DOUG.** I'm giving this to you okay.

**ED.** Fuck am I gonna do with it.

**DOUG.** Take it Ed. I'm done with it.

**ED.** You goin somewhere?

**DOUG.** I got lots of things to do.
　Big Big things.

(*They both almost makes the joke but don't.*)

**ED.** That is sad.

**DOUG.** Well

**ED.** You are sad.

**DOUG.** No-one ever said I was funny.

**ED.** That's bullshit Doug

**DOUG.** Come on Ed. I gotta.

**ED.** Okay.
　Fine.
　Sure.

　(*Pause

　**ED** takes newspaper.

　**DOUG** takes a breath.*)

**DOUG.** Don't ya wanna say anything to me?

**ED.** Nah.
　You?
　Nah

**DOUG.** Thanks Eddie.

**ED.** We can go back to the City.
　We can.

(**DOUG** *turns out.*)

**DOUG.** Ladies and Gentleman,

**ED.** Doug hold on.

**DOUG.** Allow me to introduce a great man and a wonderful comedian:

Steady Eddie from Bayridge!

(*DOUG looks to ED.*)

That's my best material ever.

Don't you think?

**ED.** Let's talk.

**DOUG.** Ed, I gotta get the fuck off this stage.

I mean, The bars are waiting for me. And I hate to disappoint, you know?

(*DOUG goes behind the curtain.*)

**ED.** (*yelling to him*) Doug get back here.

Get back here.

(*A moment.*)

**ED.** You belong here. With the old logs. With the moose. This terrible Dressing room.

Yeah fuck it all Doug Fuck the ghosts.

Fuck this place am I right?

Fuck it Doug. Fuck it all.

Doug?

Doug?

(*ED looks for DOUG. He looks in the dressing room.*

*He looks backstage.*

**DOUG** *is not there.*)

Come on Doug let's tell some jokes.

Let's see your new stuff. I'm sure you've got some great material.

You can tell some stories about how your uncle used to touch you in the bath.

We gotta good crowd here Dougie.

A good crowd.

I paid em good money.

(*to audience*)

Don't look at me like that folks, I'm trying.

*(He smiles his Big Shit Eating Grin.)*

Doug the people want to see you.

They do.

*(Now* **ED** *addresses the audience.)*

I learned all my best stuff from Doug.
How to duck.

How to get off stage.
All the good stuff.

Doug?

Anyone seen Doug?
He's hard to miss.
He's so fat that his waistline is three digits
Doug?
Where'd he go?

*(The curtain opens.*

*Only a drum.*

**ED** *fixes his hair.*

**ED** *alone on stage.*

*He picks up the drum.)*

Hey Doug?
Doug?
HEY DOUG?
Anyone seen Doug?
Doug?
BING
BING

*(The TV light comes up on* **ED**.
*It's white, blue, grainy.*
*The TV music comes on.*
**ED** *notices the audience.*

**ED** *takes a moment.*

**ED** *looks around.*

**ED** *'finds' the camera.*

*He speaks into the camera.)*

**ED.** *(super slick, TV-style)* Hey there folks welcome to our show we got a great great show for you tonight Great show.

My partner and I
My partner and I
Wait where is he?

My partner and I, we were just in the Catskills and lemme tell ya

That's rough crowd.

They're so rough.
How rough are they?
They're so rough let's just say one of us isn't around anymore.

No it's true I used to have a partner.

*(**ED** takes a moment.)*

But, I'm Really glad to be here with you people.

And here with the King of Late Night Television.

I am.
I am so glad to be with you.
And we are gonna have a GREAT TIME!

We are.
That's right well sit back.
Just sit back cause
Tonight
Tonight

Wheeeeeew

Wheeeeeew

Wheeeeeew

(**ED** *almost loses it.*)

Oh Jesus.

Fucking Jesus God.

Wheeeeewww.

Wheeeeewww.

No I'm fine.

I'm fine.

I'm good.

I got it.

You know Who I'm about to bring out?

I know you do.

The Big Guy.

There is no where I'd rather be than with him and you.

Hey there hey there hey there.

So glad you could be here tonight.

(*A Drum Roll.*)

Just sit back

(*Drum Roll…*)

Cause tonight tonight, tonight

(*Drum Roll…*)

Is the night!

(*The Drum Roll finishes.*
*Lights fade slowly.*)

**End**

# From the Reviews of
## THE JOKE...

"Sam Marks's new play, *The Joke*, is both funny and intense. Funny in that it knows and respects the craft of its protagonists, a pair of Borscht Belt comedians; intense in a way that only stand-up comics can be when no one is watching them (and sometimes even when someone is): savage, acerbic, biting, and downright feral."
- Michael Criscuolo, nytheatre.com

"A tasty two-hander by Sam Marks...A comedy team working the Catskills in the 1960s and '70s, getting few laughs while undergoing all the stresses of a doomed marriage...And just as in a marriage in which one half of the couple changes while the other stays the same, the relationship deteriorates. Allusions to a woman and to the historical context as the '60s give way to the '70s are tantalizing but not overdone; the focus stays on the two men."
- Neil Genzlinger, *The New York Times*

"The comedians' impressively dysfunctional relationship intrigues throughout, especially as the performance draws to its frank, merciless close. Theirs is a discourse of endless tryouts ("Make me laugh," Ed demands of Doug) and rejections ("Your act is shit."). Despite their sniping, the men need each other as much as Doug needs his alcohol. If we sometimes question why, it's in the same spirit that we question our own inadequate, inescapable relationships."
- Abigail Deutsch, *Village Voice*

**Also by
Sam Marks...**

# NELSON

Please visit our website **samuelfrench.com** for complete descriptions and licensing information

# OTHER TITLES AVAILABLE FROM SAMUEL FRENCH

**ADRIFT IN MACAO**
Book and Lyrics by Christopher Durang
Music by Peter Melnick

*Full Length / Musical / 4m, 3f / Unit Sets*
Set in 1952 in Macao, China, *Adrift In Macao* is a loving parody of film noir movies. Everyone that comes to Macao is waiting for something, and though none of them know exactly what that is, they hang around to find out. The characters include your film noir standards, like Laureena, the curvacious blonde, who luckily bumps into Rick Shaw, the cynical surf and turf casino owner her first night in town. She ends up getting a job singing in his night club – perhaps for no reason other than the fact that she looks great in a slinky dress. And don't forget about Mitch, the American who has just been framed for murder by the mysterious villain McGuffin. With songs and quips, puns and farcical shenanigans, this musical parody is bound to please audiences of all ages.

SAMUELFRENCH.COM

# OTHER TITLES AVAILABLE FROM SAMUEL FRENCH

## GUTENBERG! THE MUSICAL!
Scott Brown and Anthony King

*2m / Musical Comedy*

In this two-man musical spoof, a pair of aspiring playwrights perform a backers' audition for their new project - a big, splashy musical about printing press inventor Johann Gutenberg. With an unending supply of enthusiasm, Bud and Doug sing all the songs and play all the parts in their crass historical epic, with the hope that one of the producers in attendance will give them a Broadway contract – fulfilling their ill-advised dreams.

"A smashing success!"
- *The New York Times*

"Brilliantly realized and side-splitting!
- *New York Magazine*

"There are lots of genuine laughs in Gutenberg!"
- *New York Post*

SAMUELFRENCH.COM

www.ingramcontent.com/pod-product-compliance
Lightning Source LLC
Chambersburg PA
CBHW070648300426
44111CB00013B/2319